FORGOTTEN FACTS ABOUT LIFE IN THE AMERICAN COLONIES

BY KATHLEEN CONNORS

HISTORY'S FORGOTTEN FACTS

Enslow PUBLISHING

Please visit our website, www.enslow.com. For a free color catalog of all our high-quality books, call toll free 1-800-398-2504 or fax 1-877-980-4454.

Library of Congress Cataloging-in-Publication Data
Names: Connors, Kathleen, author.
Title: Forgotten facts about life in the American colonies / Kathleen Connors.
Description: Buffalo, New York : Enslow Publishing, [2024] | Series: History's forgotten facts | Includes bibliographical references and index.
Identifiers: LCCN 2023031352 | ISBN 9781978537798 (library binding) | ISBN 9781978537781 (paperback) | ISBN 9781978537804 (ebook)
Subjects: LCSH: United States–Social life and customs–To 1775–Juvenile literature.
Classification: LCC E162 .C77 2024 | DDC 973.2–dc23/eng/20230717
LC record available at https://lccn.loc.gov/2023031352

Published in 2024 by
Enslow Publishing
2544 Clinton Street
Buffalo, NY 14224

Portions of this work were originally authored by Kristen Rajczak and published as *Life in the American Colonies*. All new material in this edition authored by Kathleen Connors.

Designer: Tanya Dellaccio Keeney
Editor: Kristen Rajczak Nelson

Photo credits: Cover, series background (banners) Ledelena/Shutterstock.com; cover, series background (paper) Vitaly Korovin/Shutterstock.com; cover, series background (wood) Pataradon Luangtongkum/Shutterstock.com; cover (main) Courtesy of the New York Public Library; pp. 4 (Jamestown), 7 Morphart Creation/Shutterstock.com; p. 5 NuttyProfessor12/Shutterstock.com; p. 9 https://upload.wikimedia.org/wikipedia/commons/5/50/The_Slave_Trade_by_Auguste_Francois_Biard.jpg; p. 11 Everett Collection/Shutterstock.com; p. 13 (top) https://upload.wikimedia.org/wikipedia/commons/a/a5/1670_virginia_tobacco_slaves.jpg; p. 13 (bottom) Sara Armas/Shutterstock.com; p. 15 (left) https://upload.wikimedia.org/wikipedia/commons/a/a9/Boston_-_Old_North_Church_%2848718566608%29.jpg; p. 15 (right) https://upload.wikimedia.org/wikipedia/commons/a/a3/Old_North_Church_Boston_1882.jpg; p. 17 (both) Alexander Sviridov/Shutterstock.com; p. 19 https://upload.wikimedia.org/wikipedia/commons/8/83/New-England_Primer_Enlarged_printed_and_sold_by_Benjamin_Franklin.jpg.

Printed in the United States of America

CPSIA compliance information: Batch #CWENS24: For further information contact Enslow Publishing at 1-800-398-2504.

CONTENTS

THE BRITISH COLONIES 4
THE CHOICE TO COME 6
A LIFE OF ENSLAVEMENT 8
HARD LIVES, HARD WORK 10
WHAT'S THE WEATHER? 12
STAYING NEAR HOME 14
WHAT TO WEAR 16
SCHOOL DAYS 18
FROM COLONIES TO COUNTRY 20
GLOSSARY 22
FOR MORE INFORMATION 23
INDEX 24

Words in the glossary appear in **bold** type the first time they are used in the text.

THE BRITISH COLONIES

The British began trying to colonize, or build settlements in, North America in the 1580s. By the 1730s, Great Britain had established 13 North American colonies under its control.

JAMESTOWN, FOUNDED IN 1607, BECAME PART OF THE COLONY OF VIRGINIA.

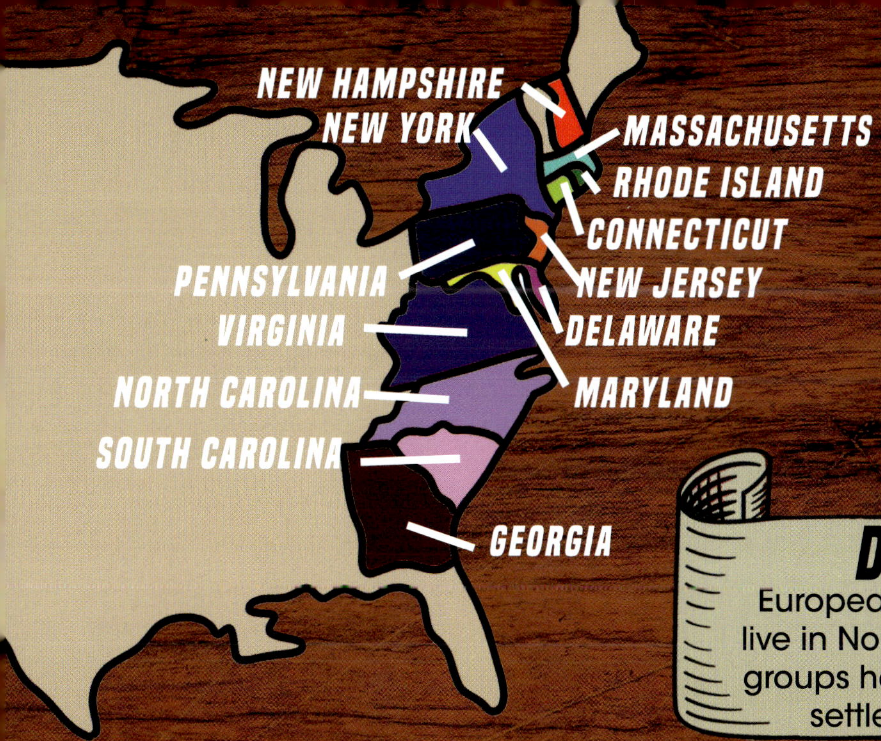

DON'T FORGET!

Europeans weren't the first people to live in North America! Native American groups had lived on the land colonists settled for thousands of years.

Some people who lived there came from Great Britain looking for a fresh start. Others were Spanish, French, and Dutch. They stayed in the New World as their countries' colonies were taken over by the British. Life differed from colony to colony, but together the colonists helped create today's American **culture**.

THE CHOICE TO COME

The colonists came for many reasons. Many colonists came to North America to escape **persecution** because of their religion, or faith. Colonists even founded some colonies for followers of a certain faith.

DON'T FORGET!

Indentured means that someone paid for a person's travel to the colonies. To pay them back, the traveler promised to work for a certain number of years.

THE PURITANS WERE ONE GROUP THAT CAME TO NORTH AMERICA FOR RELIGIOUS FREEDOM. THEY WANTED TO REFORM, OR FIX, THE CHURCH OF ENGLAND. SOME OF THEM SETTLED IN THE MASSACHUSETTS BAY COLONY, FOUNDED IN 1630.

Not all people living in the 13 colonies came by choice. The British government often shipped **criminals** from England to colonies such as Maryland as **punishment** for their crimes. Some people were forced to, or made to, become indentured servants. Others chose this as a way to get to the colonies.

A LIFE OF ENSLAVEMENT

For much of the colonial period, enslavement was allowed by law and lifelong in every colony. By the 1770s, about 500,000 enslaved people lived in the colonies.

DON'T FORGET!

Colonists also enslaved any children born to an enslaved person. This meant they often split up families when they sold a child or parent to another plantation.

ENSLAVED PEOPLE CAME FROM TRIBES ALL OVER AFRICA, MAINLY THOSE ON THE WESTERN COAST. THEIR CULTURES WERE OFTEN AS DIFFERENT FROM EACH OTHER AS THE BACKGROUNDS OF THE EUROPEAN COLONISTS.

How colonists treated enslaved people depended on where they lived. Those forced to work in southern **plantation** fields labored from sunrise to sunset. Their food and living conditions were poor. Those forced to work in homes or cities often had better food and clothing. Still, neither group had any rights. In 1777, Vermont became the first state to abolish, or end, enslavement.

HARD LIVES, HARD WORK

Survival in the colonies wasn't easy. Before 1640, colonists often died before they'd been in North America a year. One-fourth of babies didn't live to their first birthday. Colonists caught—and died from—new illnesses.

Those who lived worked hard, no matter what colony they settled in. They had to build homes and roads. They needed to learn what food grew well in their surroundings. Additionally, colonists feared attacks from Native Americans as the colonies grew.

COLONISTS OFTEN DEPENDED ON TRADE WITH NATIVE AMERICAN GROUPS, ESPECIALLY AT FIRST WHILE THEY WERE ESTABLISHING THEIR SETTLEMENTS.

DON'T FORGET!

It was common for colonists to fight with some Native American groups and be friendly with others.

WHAT'S THE WEATHER?

What colonists' lives were like had a lot to do with the **climate**. They had to find ways to deal with the hard New England winters and the terrible heat of summers in the South.

In the South, colonists built many homes with a front porch. They used this as an outdoor living space. It was cooler than staying inside! Rich southern planters might spend their summers in the North to keep out of the heat altogether.

DON'T FORGET!

Southerners wore lighter colors and **fabrics** to stay cool. Even then, they knew to drink more in the heat too.

DUE TO THE CLIMATE, FARMERS IN NEW ENGLAND HAD A SHORT SEASON TO GROW CROPS. PLANTATIONS IN THE SOUTH, LIKE THE ONES SHOWN HERE, GREW THEIR "CASH CROPS"—SUCH AS TOBACCO—ALMOST YEAR-ROUND.

STAYING NEAR HOME

People didn't travel far during the colonial period. Poorly built roads made it hard. Colonists often didn't leave their town, much less their colony. This led to differences between colonial communities. Virginia had clear social classes complete with an upper class that held most of the power. Massachusetts, on the other hand, gave everyday men more of a say.

Communities were small in both the North and South. By the 1700s, only five communities were big enough to be called cities.

OLD NORTH CHUCH
BOSTON, MASSACHUSETTS

TODAY

1882

BOSTON, MASSACHUSETTS, HAD ABOUT 15,000 PEOPLE IN IT BY 1750. IT HAD 18 DIFFERENT CHURCHES FOR ITS PEOPLE TO VISIT.

DON'T FORGET!

Many communities came together each week at church. Some colonists traveled dozens of miles to reach their church services!

WHAT TO WEAR

Some women in the colonies made their own cloth. They sewed all the clothes for their family—and fixed them when needed.

Wealthier colonial families tried to keep up with clothing styles in England. That often meant ordering clothing from London that had been shipped there from all over the world! A lady could buy a silk gown made in China for herself and a shirt made in northern Europe for her son.

DON'T FORGET!

People living in the 13 colonies were still British **citizens**!

TODAY, YOU CAN SEE COLONIAL CLOTHING AT PLACES SUCH AS THE PLIMOTH PATUXET MUSEUMS. THE PEOPLE WORKING THERE DRESS AS COLONISTS DID.

SCHOOL DAYS

What school was like for colonial kids depended on where they lived. Some went to a one-room schoolhouse to learn how to read and write. Others had a teacher, called a tutor, that came to their home. Other kids were taught by their parents.

What was taught depended largely on where a child lived too. Reading, writing, and basic math were commonly taught. In New England, knowing how to read the Bible was believed to be very important.

THE NEW ENGLAND PRIMER, **PUBLISHED** IN 1688, WAS THE MAIN TEXTBOOK USED IN THE COLONIES.

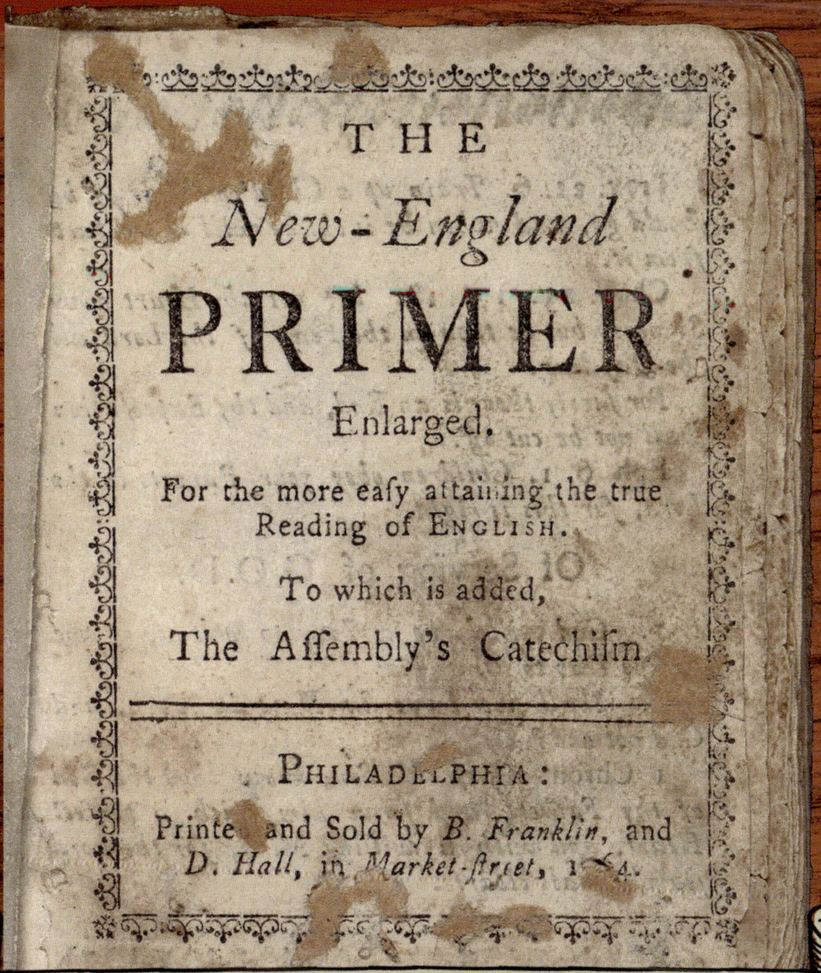

THE

New-England

PRIMER

Enlarged.

For the more eaſy attaining the true Reading of ENGLISH.

To which is added,

The Aſſembly's Catechiſm.

PHILADELPHIA:

Printe[illegible] and Sold by *B. Franklin*, and *D. Hall*, in *Market-ſtreet*, 1[illegible].

DON'T FORGET!

Colonial kids had fun too. In New York, they might go fishing, or go sledding and ice skating in the winter. In the South, colonists liked horse racing and dancing.

FROM COLONIES TO COUNTRY

The 13 North American colonies each had their own government headed by a governor who reported to the British king by the mid-1700s. Though the governor was in charge, colonists had a lot of freedom. This changed in the 1760s.

The British government needed to raise money through taxes to pay for wars it had fought. It began passing laws that angered the colonists. These laws were one main reason the colonists fought for their freedom against Great Britain in the American Revolution.

DATES TO REMEMBER

1607
JAMESTOWN, THE FIRST **PERMANENT** BRITISH COLONY, IS ESTABLISHED.

1630
THE MASSACHUSETTS BAY COLONY BEGAN TO BE SETTLED.

1664
THE BRITISH TAKE CONTROL OF THE COLONY OF NEW NETHERLAND AND RENAME IT NEW YORK.

1712
THE COLONY OF CAROLINA SPLIT INTO NORTH CAROLINA AND SOUTH CAROLINA.

1733
GEORGIA, THE LAST BRITISH COLONY, IS FOUNDED.

1776
THE 13 COLONIES DECLARE INDEPENDENCE FROM GREAT BRITAIN.

DON'T FORGET!

The American Revolution, the war for the colonies' freedom from Great Britain, began in 1775. In 1781, the United States was born when the colonists won the war.

GLOSSARY

citizen: Someone who lives in a country legally and has certain rights.

climate: The average weather conditions of a place over a period of time.

criminal: Someone who has done a crime, or something against the law.

culture: The customs, practices, and beliefs of a group of people.

fabric: A kind of cloth.

permanent: Lasting or in place a long time.

persecution: The act of treating people who are different in a harmful way.

plantation: A large farm.

publish: To put out as a book.

punishment: The act of making someone suffer for wrongdoing.

wealthy: The state of having a lot of money.

FOR MORE INFORMATION

Books

Collison, Campbell. *The Original 13 Colonies*. Minneapolis, MN: Bearport Publishing Company, 2021.

Silva, Sadie. *The Thirteen Colonies*. Buffalo, NY: Enslow Publishing, 2023.

Websites

British Empire Facts!
www.natgeokids.com/nz/discover/history/general-history/british-empire-facts/
Read more about the huge British empire the 13 colonies were part of.

Thirteen Colonies Facts for Kids
www.dkfindout.com/us/history/american-revolution/british-america-thirteen-colonies/
Review the 13 British colonies as well as facts about the American Revolution here.

Publisher's note to educators and parents: Our editors have carefully reviewed these websites to ensure that they are suitable for students. Many websites change frequently, however, and we cannot guarantee that a site's future contents will continue to meet our high standards of quality and educational value. Be advised that students should be closely supervised whenever they access the internet.

INDEX

American Revolution, 20, 21
children, 8, 10, 18, 19
clothing, 13, 16, 17
Connecticut, 5
Delaware, 5
enslavement, 8, 9
farming, 10, 13
Georgia, 5, 21
Great Britain, 4, 5, 7, 16, 20
indentured servant, 6, 7
Maryland, 5, 7
Massachusetts, 5, 7, 14, 15, 21
Native Americans, 5, 10, 11
New Hampshire, 5
New Jersey, 5
New York, 5, 19, 21
North Carolina, 5, 21
Pennsylvania, 5
religion, 6, 7, 15, 18
Rhode Island, 5
South Carolina, 5, 21
Vermont, 9
Virginia, 4, 5, 14
weather, 12, 13